MW01291658

Universal State of Mind

Lennée Reid

Cover art by Arna Baartz

ISBN 978-1544293585

www.thegirlgod.com

Some Other Girl God Books

Single Mothers Speak on Patriarchy

More than 45 single mothers from around the world share their struggles and triumphs via essays, poems, art and critique. (Includes a poem by Lennée.)

Jesus, Muhammad and the Goddess

More than 35 international contributors reflect on finding Goddess within (and without) Christianity and Islam.

The Girl God

A book for children young and old, celebrating the Divine Female. Magically illustrated by Elisabeth Slettnes with quotes from various faith traditions and feminist thinkers.

My Name is Lilith

Whether you are familiar with the legend of Lilith or hearing it for the first time, you will be carried away by this lavishly illustrated tale of the world's first woman. This creative retelling of Lilith's role in humanity's origins will empower girls and boys to seek relationships based on equality rather than hierarchy.

New Love: a reprogramming toolbox for undoing the knots

New Love is a powerful combination of emotional and spiritual techniques for women who wish to move away from patriarchal thought. This reprogramming workbook combines the wisdom of intentional visual art and inspiring words. *New Love* includes a mixture of compelling thoughts and suggestions for each day, along with a "toolbox" to help transform the parts of your life you want to heal.

www.thegirlgod.com

Table of Contents

Temple of Poetry

Welcome to the temple of poetry
Where we are initiates
In the sacred arts of
Listening and giving a shit
Our most devout would gladly
Shout truth from rooftops
We place authenticity on a pedestal
Kneel to the word in all its forms
Open chapbooks read prayers of warriors
Here we are blessed to experience life
Through the eye of another
Receive the sacraments of
Goose bumps tears and jaw drops
Be baptized in an inky blood of courage
Intolerance and ignorance are crucified here
Punctured by nails of truth
Here we are crowned
With thorns tearing our minds
So we find healing through releasing the pain
Let us resurrect this day a revolution
Blessed with information
You see the truth sanctifies from pulpits
Just like soapboxes and stages
As muses dance off the tip of tongues
Convert your heart to open
So listen when poets pour their souls
Into the cup of your mind
I thank you for spending your time here with me
In the temple of poetry

Wisdom of a Sherpa

There are many ways to reach the mountain top
One can be airlifted but that's unlikely
Still you can't pilot yourself and get out
To enjoy the view on Everest

There are many ways to climb a mountain
The path most often traveled is clear
Well known has every manner of traveler
And every peril has been overcome
See the bridges and signs for your safety

There are many paths clearly marked
But only blazing a new way on your own
Will you receive oneness with the trail
Meeting every turn the first time
Naming the rocks and streams
After learning their secrets

Many paths are walked with a friend
But truly one is either leading or following
Gaining friendship and help carrying the load
Still two pairs of feet walking where
Some places the way is only one wide
Only room for one at the top at a time

There are many ways to climb a mountain
And as many ways to fall
Sliding back through the memories
Lost at dusk
Never to be seen again

There are many ways to climb a mountain
There is only one view
Let truth be your guide
Choose your path wisely

That I Am

I am a student of prophets but
I am not a Christian or Jew
I pray to the east but not for Islam
I begin meditation with a singing bowl and mala
Yet I am not a Buddhist
My address is an apartment
Though my soul lives in a longhouse
Yearning for the comfort of a sanctuary
My cauldron is enormous
Still not entirely Pagan or Wiccan
I see with my third eye and I'm not Hindu
I breathe in and out pranayama yoga
Though I've never read the Vedas
As I fold my laundry I sing songs
Born in the hearts of slaves deep in the past
Yet my soul is free
I listen in silence and hear everything at once
I am oneness and harmony

Friends

I hope that everyone meets that friend
That no matter whether the weather
Or whether it's been

Five ten or twenty years
You're always on the same page
Know what to say to dry the tears
Across the miles you share the same cheers

You meet each other and right from day one
Create the very same beat
On the same kind of drum
You know the one

That nobody else marches to
Except me and you yes us two
Though it seems at times we are one

Top 20 Reasons I Love Cascadia

#20 Berries – – Blackberries, raspberries, salmon berries, huckleberries, Spooners strawberries... You thought I was going to say apples didn't you? Nope, the berries are better.

#19 Farmers markets with flying fish, bakeries that make soul cookies, urban farms with ancient vines, and organic locally made lollipops with zero regrets.

#18 You don't have to shovel rain. True story.

#17 "It's in the water" Best tap water this side of the Rockies.

#16 No plastic bags as of July 1st 2014 ...you environment destroying single use menaces.

#15 Pow wows – Because thankfully there are many tribes out here that survived the holocaust of colonization historically disguised as manifest destiny.

#14 I have never been called a nigger in Cascadia. At least not to my face. Or any other slur of races I am not actually but resemble enough that I catch their insults in 'Murica. We are very inclusive and tolerant out here in Cascadia, for the most part. I love that!

#13 Festivals -Cascadia Poetry Festival, The Spring Fairy Festival, Chinese new year celebrations, and PRIDE just to name a few.

#12 Rainbow Valley in the 1990's. I think I may have taken a trip there once and if I did it was not a bad one.

#11 Decent local economies sprinkled with Boeing, Microsoft, and other global diabolical badassery for good measure such as....

#10 JBLM, Bremerton and Whidbey Naval bases. Just in case TSHTF Washingtonians will be pretty safe while soldiers kick Russian ass and the best drag queens north of San Francisco sing the star spangled banner with fierceness unlike any other.

#9 TESC and Cascadia Now! They are such a cute young couple.

#8 Protests, Rallies, federal judges that uphold the constitution and other political awesomeness.

#7 Seattle Portland and Olympia – Cultural hubs with beautiful backdrops of the forests and mountains are found all over Cascadia.

#6 Canada is a very nice neighbor to the north eh?

#5 Religious tolerance with a heavy dose of eastern influence mixed in with a few hippies, vegans, yoga, witches, hummus and a sitar.

#420 It's a green region with MMJ, Cannacon and Hempfest or the right to be healthy and happy, as I like to call it.

#3 There are many alternative educational opportunities and community building organizations such as GRuB who work real miracles

#2 No Hurricanes, tornadoes, lightning storms, poisonous snakes or gators. Sometimes it's the things that aren't there that you really appreciate.

#1 Sasquatch – She's actually pretty cool once you get to know her.

Strength

I am strong like a peak
Unscathed by valley shadows

I stand tall like a tree
Overlooking misty meadows

I have courage faith and will
My trials make me stronger still

My friends and communities love I feel
By all these things I am healed

Warriors

I never knew when we set sail
I'd be the one to tell the tale
Of atrocities on the grandest scale
I am a warrior

My mother said "He's just a boy!"
Machine gun was my favorite toy
Efficient murder became my joy
I am a warrior

The screams and sounds I can't forget
The bombs the rounds the jets
The mask of stone on my face has set
I am a warrior

I held the hand of a dying man
His blood was sinking in the sand
We were brothers in the same band
I am a warrior

I am the one who gave him life
I am the one who was his wife
I am the child who cries at night
I am a warrior

The Ark of Harmony

The ark of the temple of harmony
Has gifts from all paths by twos and threes

The sanctuary is filled right up to the brim
With so much truth and love opinions can't fit in

The ways with which to feed the souls
Are rich and divine full is the ships hold

Every meaning every child seated on the floor equally
Thrones for all elders raised up supremely

Packed to the walls standing room only frequently
The ways and truths the lives shared together accepted equally

The Ark of the temple of harmony is docked right here
Waiting to launch in our hearts in each body is that clear?

It protects from all storms speaks to every ear
It is plain for those that listen and have desire to hear

Rainbows

Rainbows mean not much to me
Neither mountains rivers trees nor seas

But when rainbow rivers are everywhere
Soaring above mountain tops high in the air

When light runs in living waters fluid and bare
When in darkness paired we awake to stare

The awakened will know that time is there
They that sleep and the blind surely wont care

Signs from the Shore

Acid
It stings
Salish Sea
My feet in the water
Of the beach in Seattle
Burn like the heat of a campfire
Far too close to my skin

Base
It's smooth
Olympia bays
My hands in the water
Feet on the shore of Burfoot
Slick like extra smooth conditioner
Running down my arm into the drain

Becquerel
It boils
Sea of Japan
Nothing in the water
Off the coast of Fukushima
Melted down reactor poaches mother earth
As she screams like a lobster

Neurotoxin
It degenerates
Mississippi Delta
Shrimp in the water
Loose their eyes to dispersants
Generations of Cajun traditions
Lost like the profits of Deepwater horizon

Mni Wiconi
All of creation
Sacred Stone
Water protectors
Chopping black snakes with prayers
Tribes veterans hippies unite to fight
Multibillion DAPL desecration of dignity

H2o
It purified
Holy waters
Gone are the days
Of immersion into sacred Jordan
Bodies of living grounding fresh water
Fracking baptismal pools of cancer risk

Pollution
It's sickening
Earth our Mother
Speaks as waters flee before a tsunami
Yet still we ignore
Her signs from the shore

One Religion

The one true world religion
Well it's obvious can't you see

It is love and acceptance
Harmony in you and me

We agree on much already
Yet have a lot to learn

And yes, there are a few bad ideas
To metaphorically burn

There are no objects to worship
Of worship there are many

They help us and guide us
Holding our collective memories

Coexisting is close to missing
The most breathtaking of things

That all is one and one is all
When one accepts the truths they bring

Teams

The wolf coated sheep may as well have had armor
For she came back to the flock wiser and stronger

"And you thought I was lost" the sheep said upon returning
"They do this to us. I've seen them I'm learning"

It really doesn't matter which hide or skin or team you're in
It's just a big game it has always been

The reason we're still playing and can't seem to beat boss
Is that we did it to ourselves it is a personal loss

Defected to The Squirrels

Today I defect and join the squirrels
They live in trees without
Building permits cops jails or taxes
I have seen tree house masters
And totally agree trees make
Much better foundations than concrete
Free

Squirrels know how people are
Stay away from most of them
At least arms length
Many will hunt you kill you
Eat you run you over
Only a few ever stop say hi
Hang out and share peanuts
Free

Like we plant the forests
Not Arbor Day or Weyerhaeuser
Squirrels work hard take care of family
Adopt each other babies
Communicate with the heavens
Look up out over the forest warn
Predators are coming smoke fire storm

Squirrels see the world and speak
Plan for the future keep scatter seed
Chatter and whip their tails around yep that's me
Defected to the squirrels
Free

Nothing

I am about to ask you something you'll be surprised what it is
Please answer me this question are you sure that you exist?
I am nothing

I have climbed many mountains and crossed many seas
I have clothed the homeless nothing is me

I stand the test of time and plucked the apple from the tree
I sit and wait nothing is me

I marched with the King and sat with Gandhi
I helped free the slaves nothing is me

I took that bullet the attackers' fury
I tended the wounds nothing is me

One drop in the bucket a meaningless story
Just dust in the wind nothing is me

In the entirety of existence is it not plain to see?
Everything is one and nothing is me

Totem

The flight of a butterfly
Off of a beaver dam
Into the song of blue whale
Heard by the seal
Diving near the shore
Seen by the turtle
At home on a log
Watched over by bear
On her journey
To the waters that flow
From the source
High atop the mountain
Only accessible
By the ram
Crowned with horns
Seeking from above
Guidance of the eagle
Who's always at home
Above the storms

Soul

Your soul my child your soul please seek and find
The part of you that's neither body nor mind

Your soul my child your soul that irreplaceable part
Only upgradeable by working with the heart

Your soul my child your soul it never skips a beat
Neither nightfall nor blizzard hides its light or its heat

Your soul my child your soul listen can you hear
Be silent its speaks loudly without words or to ears

The soul sweet child the soul look can't you see
It shows us the oneness of all and eternity

The soul dear child the soul go now and taste
The sweetness of giving and truth never rots or wastes

The soul sweet child the soul can you feel it dance?
The joy the peace a solitary romance

Our souls great spirit our souls one light yet many colors
Help us paint the rainbow and shine our light on others

Re Ligio

In my religion there is no time
Nor objects to worship you will not find
False fixations for the mind

There are no taxes or fees or forms
You give what is free with it build and give more
So much more is in store for you on the other side
Of this religion of mine

And right from the very start
There is peace and joy in your heart
Lost in the dark child the light is not hard to find
In this religion of mine

Agenda Now

Awaken Muslim Christian Jew
Agnostics Atheists Palestinians Israelis
All of you brothers sisters family
Subtract division multiply peace
Become one house rising
Healing understanding mending atrocities
Stop contributing to death pain hate
Plant gardens of seeds of love conversation illuminates
The darkness of war
Halt sexism racism
One breed together stronger equally humanity
Learning to eliminate abuse cuddle more
Warm hugs desist apathy and sleeping blindness
Embrace happiness
Laziness is ignoring oppression give compassion
Cooperation is group ascension
Set intentions to be helpful
End ignorance anger
Start unity friendships community
Deliver understanding educating one another
Lend a hand up serve each other
Mend the broken cup share there is enough
Compete for the greatest trophies
Inner peace first world peace second
Only then can we achieve the goal
One temple Earth lovely home
This agenda now we must produce on our own

Freedom

I am free
As the beauty of sunshine
Warm on my face

Free
As an eagle that races
Above the clouds
Above the storms

And I have freedom
Like seeds that ride the wind
Like the soul of summer
Kissing my skin

And I am free
As a raindrop of love
In the desert of my soul
Quenching my thirst for light
As I ride through life

On waves of freedom
In oceans of abundance
Of space and time
Yes I am this
Free

On the Menu Today

The Fukushima platter is the house specialty
A delectable day glow selection sushi
Fresh and raw just like they were this morning
Eyes hemorrhaging in the Sea of Japan

The BP sampler includes whole eyeless shrimp
The perfect choice for the sleeping blind masses
Who fail to see the irony
I do recommend trying this soon
Their supply is limited

May I suggest a side of GMO chips and salsa?
Whose production and promotion use more crude
Than you and your car ever will

A limited time offer the claw less crab
Is a good choice for the helpless
And whoever else just doesn't care
Crabs can't grow claws in the gulf
Anymore

My personal favorite however
Fresh mastodon tar tar just pulled from the taiga
After the first forest fire in a million years
Opened that freezer door
This truly is a rare treat and melts in your mouth
Just like permafrost was never supposed to

All guests today also receive
A complimentary glass
Of authentic Antarctic lake water
That had been trapped for millions of years
Once word gets out demand will be high
Even at one thousand dollars a cup
The price is well worth it
That is if you will buy anything

And if you truly appreciate the finer things in life
In a private reserve we have a selection
Of aged Chernobyl cheddar
This can only be appreciated
By the most discerning palate
As it packs quite a breath taking bite

Enjoy your meal and thank you for dining
At the Millennium Shift Cafe
Bon Appétit

Eclogue to GRuB

GRuB doesn't just feed the hungry food or the youth truth
They serve up hope for the future too
Their staff walks on water
Blue and Gaffi made sure will always flow
From up cycled rain barrels
They don't just grow food on that farm or hope or futures
They grow wings on the backs of sullen angels
Once slumped over lost in despair
Now found on their knees dirt in their hair
Smiling friends everywhere
And just like disenfranchised youth with pink hair
They lifted me up
Through the dirt of a ten by ten garden plot
Next to a housing project
But then real projects happened
Around a picnic table of volunteers
In the self-esteem and sense of community we built
You see we planted and grew respect in each other
It seems they grow nothing but deep roots and wings
Because anybody who is given the opportunity to just be
At an urban farm run by old Evergreeners comes back to roost
Like a pigeon homing in on personal growth and seeds of truth
And I have the tag on my leg as proof
That's why I keep coming back giving them time and money
Because they gave me the bounty any good farm grows but
They did it to my heart mind and soul
And it won't rot or expire like things you acquire or desire
You can not go and buy GRuBs brand of food on just any old shelf
I know I had some myself

An Evergreen State of Mind

I feel divine when I smell pine
Stand and look at one needle from one tree
I wonder how this could possibly destroy me

How does a little cone grow up to fall
Take down a grid in seconds transformer and all

I have been to the canopy and I know the roots
They intertwine and connect as one owl hoots

This needle claims to be a tree in my hand
This speck says "I am the mighty Douglas. This is my land."

I believe this cone holds more than seeds
I possess a whole forest that needs not me

Fragile and unimportant at first it may seem
Before it fell to my feet journey of many stories

This tiny needle I hold fed its skyscraper home
Shady landmark under which I stand alone

With flecks of nature clinging to me
After floating from the sky rain of leaves

We are family of this forest same as the owl that hoots
I love the canopy and I know the roots

Insects

Insects I know are very old souls
Having many incarnations
Wise focused and driven
They reach their goals and destinations
The fruit of their works the world is built on
They are necessary extraordinary
Carrying more weight upon
Their back than any other
Easily bearing heavy loads
Up and down every road
They testify as they multiply
Their numbers untold
Home builders life givers
Making miracles on their backs
Insects are old souls
Nothing do they lack

Fire and Ice

She looks into his eyes as he lights the square. Something they've done enough times that their locked gaze never wavers. She passes it and puts her hand out to grab the canteen he's handing her. He filled it at the ranger station before heading out to Rainbow Cove and the Poor Cabin. A three hour trip by kayak where she did most of the talking, he did most of the rowing, and everyone did their best.

The rickety old dock they tied to was the perfect home for beautiful purple and pink starfish and jellyfish that look like fried eggs. It was home to what will be the most mouthwatering crab steaming by a fire over which hangs a cauldron of vegetable soup made with local roots. See that is part of the charm about the poor cabin. This place earned its name by the potatoes and onions that still grow in the old garden out back. Seed planted long ago by a fabled old man. Enough people and critters still visit and root around in the potatoes to turn 'em. The walking onions always find a place to keep growing in the sun. The three apple and two plum trees still bear fruit and pass for an orchard. Looks like a good year for bearing fruit after that legendary ice storm gave a good pruning to them all. And the wild raspberries which grow in the surrounding woods and are delicious if you're lucky enough to arrive when they are ready.

So, potatoes, onions, orchard, and raspberries, that's the story of the poor cabin. Remember it, you never know when you may need to find it. With the porch swing level and impeccable stone masonry from foundation to chimney, what more could one ask of a little cedar cabin in a year?

She puts the cap back on the canteen and takes a deep breath. Catching the faintest wisp of smoke on the wind from a few trees that caught heat from the tail end of a thunderstorm rolling away in the distance. Still smoldering but too wet to cause any danger. This cove is known for the gentle storms that come and go as fast as the rainbows they named it for. More awesome sounding than ram rock. Which it could have been called for all the sheep just above the timberline. Just skirting the glacier that must be hiding a pot of gold for all those rainbows.

One

We do not need 10 commandments
Just this one truth
There are no divisions we are one
One mind body soul life planet just one

So this is my plea this is my cry
If you do not understand I cannot tell you why
It is the ground under my feet
And my eye in the skies
I am one

When you see your brothers and sisters and say
Hey, how ya doing? Are you good?
Remember we are one
We all need something

Like the truth in the center
Of all the spokes in a wheel
Surrounded in hope and love
I honestly see we are one

Black white brown yellow and red
Gay straight queer square
We are all eating from the same plate
And sleeping in one bed
When we think of each other instead of fear
Accept each other as one

When you see a sick puppy
Or a wolf pack on the attack why stay back?
Can't you see we are in one condition
And behave as one?

Look at us and yourself in the mirror
Because everything is one
There are no fences cells prisons or walls
They are all a dream an illusion we are one

I am one
You are one person with one perspective
Born with one will and one tongue
At one time from one mother
Just one

If you seek the truth then you are one
If we'd all love our enemies...
Well I'd guess there would be none
Are you one?
There are no enemies in one
One mind body soul life planet just one

We are one Christian Muslim Jew
Animist Humanist Atheist Hindu
Wiccan Pagan the Zen Buddhists too
The agnostics are ahead of me here
You all knew .... there might be one
And here it is because we are one

Seeking wisdom truth and honesty
Understanding acceptance and forgiveness
Praying meditating and debating

Who has the best answer?
How to attain nirvana?
Will I be accepted in heaven?

Are we really separated by love people?
What are we arguing about?
Whatever it is the answer is we are one

Like one truth in the center
Of all the spokes in a wheel
Surrounded in hope and love
I honestly believe that we are one

Preacher and sinner one
Cops robbers judges prisoners one
Dealers addicts Bloods Crips hoes and pimps one

Soldier general president pope one
Kings queens and refugees one
Oppressors and oppressed one
Rich and homeless one

I am my temple our temple is we
Let us come together as one

If you enjoyed this book, please consider writing a brief review on Amazon or Goodreads.

Made in the USA
Monee, IL
25 September 2023

43250694R00025